Flossie

The Lucky Duck

The true story of the luckiest duck on Willow Lake

Arlene Mahlberg

ISBN: 979-8-88615-165-7 (Paperback)

         979-8-88615-166-4 (E-book)

Inks and Bindings
888-290-5218
www.inksandbindings.com
orders@inksandbindings.com

It was a bright sunny Spring morning on Willow Lake when Mr. Ben went out to his front yard to pick up his morning newspaper. As he checked the headlines on the front page, he noticed a duck fly out from one of the bushes near his mailbox. Being an inquisitive sort, Mr. Ben went to check where she had come from. Without moving any of the leaves, he saw a nest with 11 eggs in it. Wow, that mother duck was going to be a busy lady one day soon when they all hatched!

He went inside to tell Mrs. Ben about the nest and said, "We'd better keep Charlie away from the mailbox so that he doesn't frighten the mother duck away when she's sitting on her eggs." Charlie was their little Lhasa Apso who was a gentleman of a dog, but a curious sort also.

1

Every few mornings Mr. Ben would check to see if the eggs had hatched. One day he found the mother duck gone and there was only one whole egg left in the nest. There had been a big storm the night before and somehow the other eggs were all gone. Mr. Ben kept checking all that day to see if the mother duck had come back. By nightfall when she hadn't returned he was worried about that little egg, so he went into the house, logged onto his computer, and looked up what to do with a duck egg.

He found that he would have to take the mother's place and keep the egg warm. So he found a little tiny box and Mrs. Ben put some soft cotton in it and he put the egg into the box and brought it into the house. He put it into a cabinet with doors and found a small light bulb to keep it warm. He read that he had to turn the egg every 4 hours, so he set his alarm clock and got up during the night and every four hours for several days, he kept turning the egg.

Charlie would keep watch outside the cabinet and was sometimes joined by Kisse, their cat. One morning when Mr. Ben got up he saw that Charlie was wagging his tail and acting excited in front of the cabinet. Kisse was just washing his face. When Mr. Ben checked the egg box he heard a little "peep" come from inside the egg. He was so happy! The baby duck was alive!! Soon he noticed a small crack in the egg. It was beginning to hatch!!

The very next morning, Mr. Ben hurried to check the little box and he couldn't believe what he saw. The baby duck was outside the tiny broken eggshell peeping away!

Just the day before, Mrs. Ben had made a stop at the local feed store to inquire about what they would need to feed the duckling when it hatched. Mr. Jose was so helpful. He recommended a special bag of baby duck food and a bale of shaved bedding that they would need to raise the duckling for the next 4 to 6 weeks until it was ready to go into Willow Lake with all the other ducks.

So when the duckling hatched, Mr. and Ms. Ben were prepared. They put some of the feed in their hands and the little duckling began to pick it up in it's beak. They also put some water in a tiny bowl. The duckling also new to drink it. What a smart baby!

"What shall we name it?" asked Mr. Ben. Mrs. Ben thought for a minutes and said, "I think Flossie would be a good name for her! That was the name of my favorite aunt."

"But how do you know it's a girl?" asked Mr. Ben. "We don't," she answered, "but Kisse and Charlie are both boys, so I would like to think that we have another girl in the house."

So Flossie it was!! The name seemed to suit her little fluffy self too.

But now Flossie needed a larger home...the tiny little box was big enough for an egg, but now she needed room for growing and a food dish and a water dish that she couldn't tip over.

Mr. Ben went out to the garage and found a small cardboard box that he had been saving. He lined it with some old newspapers and put in the bedding that Mrs. Ben had brought home from the feed store. Then he brought it into the house and placed Flossie into it with her dishes. What a nice house she had now. Mr. Ben also kept the light bulb near her box to make sure she was warm enough.

For the next several days, Mr. and Mrs. Ben took turns making sure Flossie was eating and drinking. She was just a little puff ball but very lively and peeped when she wanted attention. She was growing so fast that they decided that someone had to teach her to swim. Mrs. Ben found a small plastic tub into which she put a few inches of warm water. They placed Flossie in the water and she liked it! She walked around in the water and splashed a bit too. So each day they added a little more water and Flossie would wade in it.

Because Flossie was growing so quickly, soon even her box was getting too small. Mr. Ben went back out to the garage and found Charlie's dog kennel. He filled it with a newspaper liner and a nice layer of bedding and brought it into the house. They needed to find bigger food and water bowls by now also. When Mr. Ben placed Flossie into the kennel, she adopted her new home immediately. But she did have one bad habit.. she kept walking into her water bowl with bedding on her feet and sitting in it. Mrs. Ben would take the bowl, wash it out and refill it with clean water and Flossie would soon sit in it again. So Mr. Ben decided it was time to find Flossie a larger place to swim. But what could they use??? The BATHTUB!! So now the family bathtub became Flossie's new swimming place. She needed the practice anyway so that she'd be ready to go into the lake in a few weeks. Flossie loved the bathtub because with deeper water that she could dive her head in and splash water all over her body.

It was such fun to watch her learn how to be a real duck. Mr. Ben thought Flossie would need to build strong legs for swimming in the lake, so he put Charlie and Kisse outside for awhile and took Flossie out of her kennel and placed her on the floor every evening. He would start walking and calling her name. She started to follow his feet and when he would change directions, Flossie would turn too.

She followed him back and forth from room to room. Her legs were growing stronger every day. Some mornings when Mr. Ben would sit in his chair and read the newspaper, he would put Flossie in his shirt pocket where she would sit contentedly for quite a while; he thought she liked the warmth of his body.

Mrs. Ben also started putting some lettuce leaves in Flossie's water bowl so she would get used to eating vegetation along with her duck food. Flossie really liked lettuce!

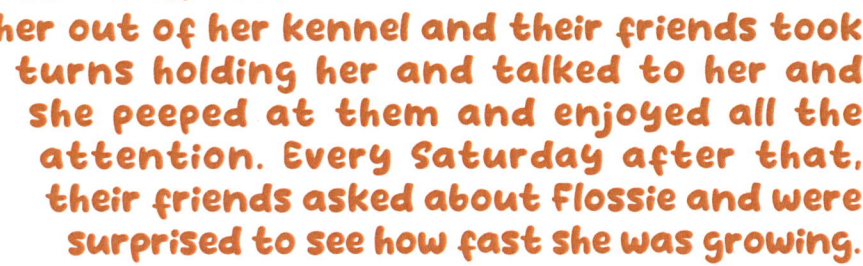

On Saturdays, Mr. and Mrs. Ben had friends over to play cards. When they heard Flossie's story they wanted to see her. So Mr. Ben took them into the guest bedroom where Flossie was, took her out of her kennel and their friends took turns holding her and talked to her and she peeped at them and enjoyed all the attention. Every Saturday after that, their friends asked about Flossie and were surprised to see how fast she was growing.

A few weeks later, it was time for Mr. and Mrs. Ben to go on their vacation. The lady, Jenny, who came to take care of Charlie and Kisse, said she would be happy to take care of the baby duck too. Flossie was almost grown big enough to go into the lake, but not quite she hadn't been able to fly yet. So Mr. Ben built her a play yard on their sandy beach under the big tree by the lake. It was an 8ft by 8ft fenced yard with a gate that Mr. Ben covered with some left-over latticework he had under his deck.

This made sure that Flossie would be safe inside while they were on vacation. Inside the yard, be put the dog kennel for her to sleep in at night, and really large tub of water for her to swim in during the day and her food and water bowls. When Mr. Ben put her into the yard, Charlie sat outside and talked to her and she quacked back at him which sounded like, "Charlie, come see my new home...there's lots of room and it's really nice in here." Kisse just rolled around in the sand outside the yard and really didn't pay much attention at all.

15

Flossie grew bigger and stronger every day and the other ducks on the lake would swim by and quack at her and tell her they were waiting for her to come on and swim with them. One day, Jenny went out to put fresh water and food in Flossie's bowls and discovered Flossie was gone! She found a small trench dug under the fence near the lake. There were duck tracks leading from the fence to the edge of the lake.

Flossie's duck friends must have convinced her to join them in the lake! The very next day Mr. and Mrs. Ben returned from vacation. They were surprised to find Flossie had found a way out of her yard, but the very next morning, bright and early, Mr. Ben walked out onto his dock and called, "Flossie." From the island across the lake, a little duck started swimming towards the dock. Mr. Ben was so excited to see her. He knew it was Flossie because she swam right up to the dock and he recognized her white tail feathers. He threw some small pieces of bread wrapped around the duck food into the lake and Flossie gobbled them up. She seemed just as happy to see him as he was to see her.

Flossie came back three times every day: morning, noon and evening to see Mr. Ben and get her duck food treats. Sometimes, she even brought some of her new duck friends. They liked the treats too but wouldn't come up as close to the dock as Flossie did. Mr. Ben began to recognize them by their feather colors.

Then a few weeks later, she came by and flapped her wings as if to say "goodbye, it's time for me to fly off now....it's getting cooler here and my friends want me to fly south with them. I'll be back next Spring, Mr. Ben. Thanks for everything! I love you!."

Mr. & Mrs. Ben were sorry to see her go, but knew that was why they had raised her so carefully, so that she could be independent and safe in her duck world.

Winter went by quickly and soon it was Spring again. Mr. Ben kept looking to see if Flossie was back yet....one day, he saw some Mallard ducks back on the lake...he was so excited...he called "Flossie, Flossie." But no one swam towards the dock. Every day he would go out to the dock and call. A few weeks later, when he did this, much to his delight, a female and a male duck came swimming up to the dock...it could be Flossie...Sure enough, she came really close to the dock and even jumped up onto it...her male companion joined her for the treats Mr. Ben would give them.

21

Mrs. Ben asked the grandchildren, "What should we name Flossie's husband?" They thought that Frank would be a perfect name. So Frank it is!

Now each Spring, Mr. Ben looks for Flossie, and sure enough she returns to his dock with Frank. Frank is quite the gentleman, he lets Flossie have her fill of treats before he eats some himself. They even jump up onto the deck and come up to the door if Mr. Ben is late with his treats. They are the only two ducks on the whole lake that are so friendly. Mr. & Mrs. Ben enjoy seeing them and hope that this will be the year Flossie brings her baby ducks by for them to meet.